HAP:
Understudies of Thomas Wyatt's Petrarch
Robert Sheppard

*All the King's wives and all the King's Men
Couldn't put Wyatt together again*

Newton-le-Willows

Published in the United Kingdom in 2018
by The Knives Forks And Spoons Press,
51 Pipit Avenue,
Newton-le-Willows,
Merseyside,
WA12 9RG.

ISBN 978-1-912211-20-3

Copyright © Robert Sheppard, 2018.

The right of Robert Sheppard to be identified as the author of this work has been asserted by them in accordance with the Copyrights, Designs and Patents Act of 1988. All rights reserved. No part of this publication may be reproduced, stored in a retrieval system, transmitted in any form or by any means, electronic, photocopying, recording or otherwise, without prior permission of the publisher.

Acknowledgements

Some of these poems have appeared in the following magazines: *Blackbox Manifold*, *Poetry at Sangam*, *International Times*, and in *For Robert: An Anthology* (RHUl Poetics Research Centre/Crinoline Editions, June 2017.

Hap:
Understudies of Thomas Wyatt's Petrarch

TABLE OF CONTENTS

Perhaps a Mishap   7

Hap 1
Som fowles there be that have so perfaict sight   8

Hap 2
How oft have I, my dere and cruell foo   9

Hap 3
Because I have the still kept fro lyes and blame   10

Hap 4
Ever myn hap is slack and slo in commyng   11

Hap 5
Was I never yet of your love greved   12

Hap 6
Caesar, when that the traytor of Egipt   13

Hap 7
Love and fortune and my mynde, remembre   14

Hap 8
I find no peace and all my war is done   15

Hap 9
Who so list to hounte I knowe where is an hynde   16

Hap 10
The longe love, that in my thought doeth harbar   17

Hap 11
Suche vayn thought as wonted to myslede me   18

Hap 12
Me thynkethe my head is with childe, alas!   19

Hap 13
Auysing the bright bemes of these fayer lyes   20

Hap 14
Yf amours faith, an hert vnfayned   21

Hap 15
My galy charged with forgetfulness   22

Hap Hazard   23

Resources   25

Perhaps a Mishap

Inside the poem is another poem; inside that another.
The SS guards stoop to pat the *lager* hound.
You hate the poem, its logic, its symmetries.
Somewhere, someone is giving birth on an oily rag.

They've taken a convoy of Mercedes to visit the ruins,
the diktats of a lasting piece, the master plan.
Inside the plan is another plan; you're running
through the forest with a stolen hard drive.

The dry shells of dream open as you wake – you find
no trace of relational interference. As Wyatt knows,
debugging his devices against the infant's cry,
the yearning whine of the washing machine. On

the commute from Kent he scopes the news; the fisted spider
that dissembles as a berry: one side ripening, the other rotting.

25th November 2016

Robert Sheppard

Hap 1

Som fowles there be that have so perfaict sight

I pull down the blind on the sunny train to shield my eyes
like it's 1948 and I'm some old bird from 'the firm'
deigning to meet my dark mistress in daylight
but settling for some jazz-sweaty basement in Soho again.
I blinked at Los Alamos just in time, I'd think,
to save my sight and salve my conscience;
I signed the Official Secrets Act in black and white.

But it's 2017 and out of my reverie I'm up to town
to discuss exit strategies with the three jokers.
When Boris, swollen and unstable, asks me,
'Is there anything in this Putin-Trump-Brexit business?'
I'll say, 'Nothing,' when I'd meant to say nothing,
and I'll leap from the frying pan of my *amour-propre*
into the raging fire of his blinding ambition.

Hap 2

How oft have I, my dere and cruell foo

I hold my enemies closer than the others.
And that includes you, my dear, as we negotiate exits
from our customs union! I bow, and I scrape the floor
of your bejewelled boudoir with my silvery tongue.

This could end up with my vital organs dripping lard,
packed in attaché cases and dumped in the Thames;
or me zipped up neatly folded whole in a holdall
by an attaché from the Russian Embassy. Call that

that! I'll face this exile, banishment to Kent,
holed up alone all winter in a dead resort, a sort of spy
bleaching my back story to a blank sheet, fresh start.

I'd watch Trump's inauguration on a wobbling telly:
his thumbs, swollen with promises, up. Your pain is not my gain.
Even those back-stabbing Tories dub this 'a lose-lose scenario'.

Robert Sheppard

Hap 3

Because I have the still kept fro lyes and blame

My tongue is rigid, moist in attentive silence, unlike
those of slack Brexiteers who promised the riches of the land
to a sequacious populace without delivery or deliverance.
(Wordless, it glistened down drifting down from your navel.)

Your slim leather gloves slap to the floor of the crowded train
at the feet of a young man who ignores them under his phone.
'This isn't what we wanted Feminism for,' stooping, lame;
'I just wanted the right to an abortion if I were ever raped!'

Your rights could become wrong at the flick of a tongue,
and I'd have to stand, hands behind back, tongue-tied,
beetroot-flushed at blatant bloviation, unperfected

in my studied 'Foreign Office' *sprezzatura;* minding
my mistress in Camberwell with her proofs of the next Mantell,
my wife and kids with the washing machine back in Kent.

Hap 4

Ever myn hap is slack and slo in commyng

Whatever happens happens. Slack comings or
stern desire. I'll take it or leave it. She loves me
not. These paper jousts of the pastime tiger
make brittle kindling for a heartless fire.

So snow shall rest unmelting on her black hair;
the Atlantic shall drain to leave a Grand Canyon
for our special relationship; the crowded Thameslink south
shall be free of their spy crouched behind *The Sun*;

before I shake off this sweat of conspiracy, this
fear of wrongful arrest (and the rest). I'm as bitter and twisted
as Kentish beer – culpable sweetness covers her winy secrets,

saccharine wasteland where I build my shanty trust,
a refugee camp that I can no longer police – now I arrive.
I'm wired, wired-up, Wyatt. Anything could happen.

Robert Sheppard

Hap 5

Was I never yet of your love greved

A dead file with your name on it (and mine)
could finish me off, just as I'm commissioned
to speak in *propria persona*. No longer aping
Petrarch or Plutarch for the first first lady,

I'm filing a report to frame the second's dark portrait.
I'm impelled to dredge the linings of Eurocrats' stomachs,
with a posting to Brussels in the last days should I fail.
On the last night the umbrella tip might sting my vitals.

Don't touch me! I shall persist, though you insist on tears
(mine). You're right on rights, the environment, nukes, yet
you're squawking like one of Trump's tweets in CAPS!

Cause and effect is affected by metatruths and his dispatches
but you'll only bring the flat (or the axe) down on your head:
you're the last cause of everything I hold dear, LOSER!

Hap 6

Caesar, when that the traytor of Egipt

Theresa, when grasped by the tiny hand of the tyrant,
presented on a plate the guts of the NHS, and smiled,
as his long red tie tickled his glans, though she sweated
beneath a grand's worth of leather trousers, unaroused.

I jetted trans-Alpine to our 'European allies' with friable promise.
If only I could rope Remoaner Reginald Pole to the pole,
slop inflammable beard balm over his hipster bush, my eyes
watering at the garlicky aroma of barbequed traitor, and

disgorge my stomach as he blisters! Duplicitous spider am I:
her fake furs and my fake news brushed smooth and receptive
to time and season, de-briefing, and briefing, on fake leather couches.

No other way to say this, so I don't: We must quit loving!
She grabs me by the man-pussy and I roll over into deceit's
thick web: I'll tell anything, promise everything.

Robert Sheppard

Hap 7

Love and fortune and my mynde, remembre

I'm taking the rap (again) between these sheets (alone)
or undercover in Brussels. My mind presents present promise
against the presence of the past, which is expiring faster than
my EU passport. (When I speak like that I wish I were dead.)

I'm out of sorts (with love, with you), and the *failing* pound
leaves me out of pocket here after one sour greuze and,
out of my mind, I crank myself up in the middle of the night,
to rub out my heretic Reginald like a furious youth!

Pleasure is a gif file on repeat: your breasts swinging.
All I'll bring back from Europe will be re-memories of England.
I'll be through these hapless sonnets before we hit the worst.

My fortunate face peppers with glass, my untrue heart splintered:
iron discipline shatters the one-way mirror during illicit interrogation,
its evidence as inadmissible as happiness.

Hap 8
I find no peace and all my war is done

'I am a difficult poet in Kent' (Charles Bernstein)

I jet above the world's woolly defence. My hubris clouds over.
I've been withdrawn from Brussels. Draw no conclusions from *The Daily Hate*.
I've nothing in my diplomatic bag, yet all of Europe fructifies beneath;
I fear I'll be frozen out from Boris, dried out in Frinton again.

Love of my country (and *her*) loosened my tongue, but now
I'm as tight as a berry. I'm unsafe in this safe house,
dark space for my dark place, like Pole's mum on the block
when her head went *splat! splat! splat!* ha-ha.

I'm fixed in Brexitland permafrost, purr warm words about soft power.
I'm the Baptist of a British Anthropocene, the Commonwealth of Big Data.
I love it all, yet my wife alone loves the washing machine man, a Pole.

I pull the wrong face in the wrong sonnet and it weeps ha-ha.
This unreformed pleasure is the cause of my back-pocket
schadenfreude: Paul Nuttall's fake degree from Edge Hill.

Robert Sheppard

Hap 9

Who so list to hounte I knowe where is an hynde

Once I chased you round your flat, dear heart,
and we fucked like rabbits until we were sore; or,
spread on your Field of the Cloth of Gold bedspread, you spread;
or rose, wild, to be mounted, and I came from behind.

I thought of that moment before (in Brussels): when
your loose gown fell from your shoulders, but you slipped
naked through my toils to your toilet, fishnets void.
I served up this reverie of service to myself.

You other me into the last lover on your long list;
I spy through your bedroom keyhole: you service yourself
with your G-spot rabbit, and your felt-tip banner from

the Anti-Trump March teases: *KEEP YOUR HANDS OFF
MY REPRODUCTIVE RIGHTS!* You are your own lover first.
'This *last* time,' you say, 'I'll tie you up and toss you off!'

Hap 10

The longe love, that in my thought doeth harbar

Length is measured by my wife's receptivity.
She holds *him* close with his in-your-face toolbox,
his bulging bag of bolts, his lengthy wrench.
His white van parks in her drive. She spreads

ambassadorial safe conduct for this envoy of joy!
Trust him to pull himself, and lust's negligee, off.
His hard thrust celebrates the National Insurance U-
turn. He takes *her,* but who takes the photograph?

Back early, I find them arranged as on the *Punting
in Kent* Twitterfeed that Gove had notified me of:
gaping bacon pulsed upon her washing machine top.

I'll sliver his liver! Across the shire he speeds in his
fishnet codpiece, hiding in oasthouses and dogging sites.
But first, I'll slash his tyres and send for the crusher.

Robert Sheppard

Hap 11
Suche vayn thought as wonted to myslede me

Lost in the deserted estates of East Kent, I live
alone with my vanity project – translations of lost
sonnets – absented from PM, and wife, and mistress:
disgraced by the first; the wife cast out in shame;

the clean break with my mistress's dirty love (but the loss
of her dodgy intel). She won't pick up: I cast myself down
on the couch. On TV I watch the terror attack
at Westminster, lockdown of the palace of liberty,

from where May promised to mend our broken shires
but stumbles now over a homily to human rights. Amid
the broken bodies all I see is *her* lost face, like thunder,
electric lightning sex, compressed code – cold comfort

as they come for me, at last. Recalled from unquiet
solitude, emboldened by accusation, I cry, *Bring it on!*

Hap 12

Me thynkethe my head is with childe, alas!

I frame my defence in the dark tower
but my words disappear as they are written.
The sticky fog of accusation licks at my heels
and I stumble, lashing out at my shadow.

Headache fills this cell: heartache fuels the world.
Unsheath my poison pen. My rapier wit slashes
against these slash-stained walls. This sonnet is as fake
as the witness is false – *and* as the dream I lose you in.

I awake in a modern office, wire chairs in an oval:
the complainant's script flaps like a tongue on his lap.
My stab at the State Bard proves inadmissible and

I'm freed. But the next time the boss says to me
All my wives looked like Honeysuckle Weeks,
I'll just smile, enigma's secret groom.

Robert Sheppard

Hap 13

Auysing the bright bemes of these fayer lyes

Look at the glowering greed in their eyes.
Many (almost most) weep to hear the Trigger triggered
while talk of 'Henry VIII powers' taxes the dirty mind
in a Kentish paradise of 'villages and hamlets' where
guys in slacks sip bitter and compare the legs
of Mrs May and Nicola Sturgeon.

Between misery and wealth, principle and ambition,
few are glad, and the Many have no Plan B (or A): but
soft Regrexit for Hard Brexit as repealers unspin.

Espy through Edenic cobwebs of gardening leave
spun across the complaints and appeals procedures,
those frost cravings delivered to Bruxelles on spurs of fire.

Brought to such extremes thought freezes
though its bearer stoops unthinking into flame.

Hap 14

Yf amours faith, an hert vnfayned

If honesty bubbles on the hob unboiled
If mad policy tempered by my diplomatic tweaks
breeds festering slough thwarted desire
If you think less of the electorate than of the elect
If the Brexiteer's battle-bus with its cashback payback
U-turns on a blind corner (as IDS pleads to camera!)
If every thought (Quiet Wyatt!) cartoons on my brow
as my croaky voice now gruff now falsetto (and false!)
blurts or tweets the alt. facts bare-faced for you
If Bojo's 'piccaninny' show is hardly worth blacking up for
If wailing sirens on Westminster Bridge burn sorrow into anger
If feverishness for athletic tricks freezes out my old mistress
If I am destroyed by love riding hard
the fault is mine the irredeemable convenience yours.

Robert Sheppard

Hap 15

My galy charged with forgetfulness

My Harley Low Rider charges without a doubt
across the potholed tarmac of Austerity;
steering between my rock and their hard place,
I roar helmeted, Boris still forgetful of my loyalty.

Every piston of this mid-life-crisis indulgence
fires me on towards my death. Torqued to the asphalt,
I fart my way over bumpy hillocks, a boil on my butt.
(But who took the photo? Who 'suggested' he 'send for' me?)

Blanket cloud, sheet rain, on the M20. The spray from
Euro-lorries tests my skidding, and I swerve, and yet
still I serve, despite my confessed 'error', their half-truths.

I no longer read the starry messages I courier across Christendom
and Kent. Drenched in shame beyond reason: I stand,
deliver the 'goods', then tear up the back roads to Nowhereland.

January – April 2017

Hap Hazard

This poem is the un-perished part of another,
and behind that, the other poem, the one in foreign,
as behind Theresa May there squats the succubus
of Thatcher, donning the rubber masks of Englishness.

From east to west Wyatt charges on his Harley;
from brunette to blonde he changes his like to true Anglo,
thundering sparkplugs and sparkling blue eyes.
Wobbling, he'll only live for six more English lines.

His pen admonishes the knaves of Kent, caught dallying
with 'lactating maids' at Maidstone. In plaintive woe,
he issues this feverish prophecy of his unquiet mind:

'They're all struck dumb by May's lightning election call:
Corbyn at stool, Boris mid-bullying, his Bullingdon bull,
all her enemies routed in one swift English retreat.'

(for Robert Hampson)

April 2017

Resources

Brigden, Susan. *Thomas Wyatt: The Heart's Forest*. London: Faber and Faber, 2012.

Muir, Kenneth. ed. *Sir Thomas Wyatt: The Collected Poems*. London: Routledge and Kegan Paul, 1949.

Rebholtz, R.A. ed. *Sir Thomas Wyatt: The Complete Poems*. Harmondsworth: Penguin, 1978.

Shulman, Nicola. *Graven with Diamonds: The Many Lives of Thomas Wyatt*. London: Short Books, 2011.

Thomson, Patricia. *Sir Thomas Wyatt and His Background*. Stanford: Stanford University Press, 1964.

www.ingramcontent.com/pod-product-compliance
Lightning Source LLC
Chambersburg PA
CBHW031509040426
42444CB00007B/1273